CW00525367

English C1 Vocabulary 2022

The Most Comprehensive Advanced
English Vocabulary

(5th Edition)

by Premier English Learning Publishing

From the Publisher

5th edition of the most comprehensive Advanced English vocabulary. For this edition we have added more than a hundred new words.

In this book, we have collected all Advanced English words you should know to brilliantly pass writing and speaking parts of all International English Tests.

This vocabulary contains only the most important words with clear and simple definitions and up-to-date example sentences.

Study at home or in class, bookmark pages, and remember that repetition is the key to memory.

Vocabulary

Abdicate

Meaning: To give up (power, duties, obligations); to retire.

Example: The abdication of the Queen.

Abet

Meaning: To assist or encourage someone to do something illegal.

Example: She abetted the thief.

Abhor

Meaning: To strongly hate something.

Example: I abhor scammers.

Abnegation

Meaning: To deny or reject something (like a doctrine or belief); self-denial.

Example: Abnegation of political power.

Abscond

Meaning: To leave hurriedly and secretly; to run away.

Example: Prime suspect absconded to Mexico.

Abstruse

Meaning: Difficult to understand.

Example: Abstruse essay on quantum physics.

Abysmal

Meaning: Very bad or low in quality.

Example: The quality of his work is abysmal.

Accede

Meaning: To express approval; agree to do what you are asked.

Example: The government did not accede the requests of the citizens.

Accolade

Meaning: When someone is given an award or privilege to recognize their merit.

Example: My teacher received an accolade for his scientific work.

Accretion

Meaning: An addition to something.

Example: The house was expanded by the accretion of new outbuildings.

Accumulation

Meaning: A gathering or increase of something; growth by addition.

Example: Her goal for the coming year is to accumulate a large sum of money.

Acquaint
Meaning: To give someone information about something; to make familiar.
Example: We need to acquaint him with our goal.

Acrimonious
Meaning: Full of anger; bitter or harsh in manner or speech.
Example: Acrimonious debate about air pollution.

Act up
Meaning: To behave badly or oddly.
Example: The car's engine began to act up.

Acuity
Meaning: The ability to think, see, or hear very clearly.
Example: Visual acuity; political acuity.

Acumen
Meaning: The ability to make correct decisions or judgments.
Example: He has extraordinary financial acumen.

Adjacent
Meaning: Next to; nearby.
Example: Adjacent buildings; adjacent suburbs.

Adjure
Meaning: Order someone to do something.
Example: I adjure you to tell me the truth.

Adorn
Meaning: To make something more beautiful; to decorate.
Example: She loves to adorn the Christmas tree with her family.

Adroit
Meaning: Proficient; skillful.
Example: He became adroit in investing.

Adulterate
Meaning: To make something impure or weaker by adding something else.
Example: The beer had been adulterated with water.

Adumbrate
Meaning: To give the main points or summary of; to outline.
Example: The objectives of my dissertation were adumbrated on the first page.

Adversity

Meaning: An unfavorable turn of events; unlucky situation.

Example: He showed courage in the face of adversity.

Affable

Meaning: Friendly; easy to communicate.

Example: She was extremely affable on our first date.

Affectation

Meaning: Dishonest and insincere behavior or speech.

Example: Calling everyone 'sweetheart' is just an affectation.

Affluent

Meaning: Rich; wealthy; have a lot of money.

Example: Affluent nation; affluent people.

Afoot

Meaning: Being planned; in the process of development.

Example: Big changes are afoot at our city.

Agile

Meaning: Ability to move freely and quickly; ability to successfully and quickly deal with changes.

Example: He is such an agile climber.

Aggrandize

Meaning: To make greater or more powerful.

Example: The Queen sought to aggrandize her dynasty.

Ajar

Meaning: Slightly open.

Example: She had left the door ajar.

Alacrity

Meaning: Quickly; with enthusiasm; eagerly.

Example: He accepted my money with alacrity.

Albeit

Meaning: Even though; although.

Example: I tried, albeit without much success.

Amalgamate

Meaning: To unite; to bring together.

Example: Our firm has amalgamated with a British company.

Ambiguous

Meaning: Uncertain; having more than one possible meaning; doubtful.

Example: Her response to my proposal was somewhat ambiguous.

Amenable

Meaning: Easily persuaded; suggestible; manageable.

Example: Amenable children; amenable to argument.

Amend

Meaning: To make minor changes (mostly to the text) in order to improve or make better.

Example: Amend the constitution; amend the law; amend my way of living; amend the plan.

Amicable

Meaning: Friendly; peaceable; agreeable.

Example: Her behavior was amicable.

Anticipate

Meaning: To expect or predict that something will happen.

Example: We anticipate sales to pick up next week.

Aplomb

Meaning: Confident and relaxed, especially in difficult situations.

Example: He overcame difficulties with his usual aplomb.

Apocryphal

Meaning: Something that is most likely not true, but many people believe it to be true.

Example: Apocryphal stories; apocryphal sagas.

Appease

Meaning: Make peace with someone by giving them what they want.

Example: She tried to appease her little sister by giving her candies.

Apprise

Meaning: Inform someone about something.

Example: We will apprise you the results of your test.

Aquiver

Meaning: Trembling or shaking, mostly due to strong emotions.

Example: The breathtaking news set me aquiver.

Arbitrary

Meaning: Random; based on chance or personal preference.

Example: An arbitrary decision; an arbitrary choice.

Arcane

Meaning: Mysterious; secret.

Example: Arcane knowledge; arcane details of the agreement.

Archetype
Meaning: Typical or perfect example of something.
Example: Achilles is the archetype of the warrior.

Arduous
Meaning: Extremely difficult or hard; involves a lot of effort.
Example: Arduous work; arduous climb; arduous world tour.

Arid
Meaning: Dry (referring to the land or climate); uninteresting and boring.
Example: Sahara Desert is arid; his book is extremely arid.

Arouse
Meaning: To evoke or cause an emotion or particular feeling.
Example: Arouse a big laugh; arouse anger; arouse deep suspicion.

Artfully
Meaning: Demonstration of art, intelligence, or skill.
Example: Her shoes were artfully arranged in color hues.

Asinine

Meaning: Blunt; silly; stupid.

Example: Asinine remarks; asinine idea.

Assertion

Meaning: Claim that something is true; statement that you believe is true.

Example: His assertion is not supported by real evidence.

Assiduous

Meaning: Persistent; attentive to detail; caring.

Example: An assiduous student; assiduous in learning; assiduous research.

Assuage

Meaning: To make unpleasant feelings less painful or strong.

Example: A nurse can assuage someone's pain with medication.

Assume

Meaning: To accept or believe that something is true (without any proof).

Example: I assume everyone has a T-shirt.

Astounding

Meaning: Shocking; impressive; surprising.

Example: Astounding news; astounding result; astounding career.

Astute
Meaning: Able to see and react to various situations intelligently and quickly.
Example: Astute business decisions; astute investor.

Austere
Meaning: Extremely simple; plain.
Example: My father is a very austere man.

Avail
Meaning: To be of use; advantage; benefit.
Example: All our efforts did not avail.

Avarice
Meaning: Greedy desire for wealth and money.
Example: His avarice caused him to sell his father's house.

Avid
Meaning: Doing something as much as possible; very enthusiastic.
Example: He is an avid reader of short fantasy stories.

Axiomatic
Meaning: Unquestionable; obviously true.
Example: An axiomatic truth; axiomatic fact.

Banter
Meaning: Good-humored and friendly conversation.
Example: Two old friends bantered with each other.

Bashful
Meaning: Shy; easily embarrassed.
Example: He was too bashful to talk about his feelings.

Bash out
Meaning: To produce something quickly without much preparation.
Example: He bashed out about nine books a year.

Befuddle
Meaning: To confuse; make it impossible to think clearly.
Example: She was befuddled by a bottle of wine.

Beguile
Meaning: To charm or persuade someone, especially by saying nice words to them.
Example: He beguiled the voters with his big promises.

Belittle

Meaning: Make someone or something look unimportant.

Example: We should not belittle his achievements.

Belligerence

Meaning: Willingness to fight; aggressive and warlike behavior.

Example: She had a problem with her boyfriend's belligerence.

Benevolent

Meaning: Friendly; kind; helpful.

Example: Benevolent old man.

Bereft

Meaning: Lacking something.

Example: Bereft of inspiration; bereft of hope.

Bewilder

Meaning: Confusing; difficult to understand.

Example: She was bewildered by her son's reaction.

Blare

Meaning: Make loud and annoying sounds.

Example: Blare of broken speakers; blare of trumpets.

Boil up

Meaning: Experience a strong negative emotion.

Example: Anger was boiling up inside me.

Bombastic

Meaning: Trying to impress other people by saying things that sound impressive but don't mean much.

Example: The politician spoke in a bombastic manner.

Bone up

Meaning: Study hard; learn as much as possible about something.

Example: I need to bone up on my French grammar for a test on Monday.

Boon

Meaning: Helpful; beneficial; something that is asked.

Example: The rain was a boon to the withered crops.

Boondoggle

Meaning: Spend a lot of time and money, but achieve nothing; an unnecessary project.

Example: Our investments in oil were boondoggle.

Boorish

Meaning: Rude; bad-mannered; not caring about other people's feelings.

Example: Boorish behavior; boorish manner; he was very boorish.

Brackish
Meaning: Unpleasant; nasty; salty.
Example: Brackish water; brackish personality.

Brazen
Meaning: Done very openly and shockingly without shame; audacious.
Example: Brazen cheating; brazen lie; brazen love affairs.

Brooding
Meaning: Something that makes you feel uncomfortable or anxious, like something bad is about to happen.
Example: A brooding silence; brooding over what to do next.

Brusque
Meaning: Quick, unfriendly, and rough in manner or speech.
Example: The doctor spoke in a brusque tone.

Burgeon
Meaning: Develop; expand or grow rapidly.
Example: He burgeoned into a perfect doctor.

Bustling

Meaning: Noisy and full of activity.

Example: Bustling market; bustling streets.

Cajole

Meaning: Convince or persuade someone to do something by being kind to them or making false promises.

Example: She knows how to cajole people into doing what she wants.

Camaraderie

Meaning: Trust and friendship between people who spend a lot of time together; sociability; feeling of friendliness.

Example: I really like the camaraderie in our team.

Canny

Meaning: Smart and able to think quickly, especially in business.

Example: Canny investors; canny marketing; canny lawyer.

Cantankerous

Meaning: Bad-tempered; argue a lot.

Example: A cantankerous old man.

Cast aspersions
Meaning: Abusive attack on a person's reputation or good name.
Example: I want to cast aspersions on my political opponent.

Castigate
Meaning: To criticize someone; to speak angrily.
Example: John never missed an opportunity to castigate the rich.

Cavil
Meaning: Arguing or complaining about unimportant details.
Example: A customer caviled about new price.

Cessation
Meaning: Stopping or ending something.
Example: A cessation of Christmas sales.

Chide
Meaning: Talking angrily to someone because they did something stupid or bad.
Example: He chided her for bad manners.

Circumlocution
Meaning: Using more words than necessary instead of speaking directly; indirect way of speaking.

Example: A circumlocutory reply; diplomatic circumlocutions.

Circumspect
Meaning: Careful; unwilling to take risks.
Example: He is very circumspect in future actions.

Clandestine
Meaning: Planned or done secretively.
Example: Our group held yearly clandestine meetings.

Cliffhanger
Meaning: A very exciting ending to a part of a book or TV show.
Example: TV drama series ends on a cliffhanger.

Cloying
Meaning: Too sweet and therefore unpleasant.
Example: The film's cloying sentimentality.

Clumsy
Meaning: Not careful; without skill; awkward in movement.
Example: The first computers were hard and clumsy to use for casual consumers.

Clunky
Meaning: Solid; old-fashioned; large.
Example: A clunky gold ring.

Coercion
Meaning: Use force to convince someone to do something they don't want to do.
Example: The police used coercion.

Cogent
Meaning: Reasonable; persuasive; logical; strong; convincing.
Example: Cogent arguments; cogent evidence.

Coherent
Meaning: Logically connected; well planned.
Example: A coherent strategy; coherent plan.

Coincide
Meaning: Occur at the same time or in the same period; be the same or similar.
Example: I timed my vacation to coincide with my wife's; my ideas coincide with hers.

Commence
Meaning: To begin something; to start.
Example: They commence their new project.

Commensurate

Meaning: Equal in significance; corresponding in size.

Example: His salary must commensurate with his skills and experience.

Compunction

Meaning: A guilty feeling about doing something.

Example: She had lied to him without compunction.

Concede

Meaning: Unwillingly admit that something is true.

Example: She was forced to concede that he was right.

Conciliation

Meaning: The action of ending a disagreement.

Example: All attempts at conciliation failed and the debate continued.

Concomitant

Meaning: Something that happens with something else and is related, connected, or associated with it.

Example: Loss of memory is a concomitant of old age.

Condescending

Meaning: Treating someone as if you are more important, better, or smarter than them.

Example: The teacher is condescending towards the students.

Condolence
Meaning: Expression of sympathy when someone has recently died.
Example: David sent him a letter of condolence because of his brother's recent death.

Connive
Meaning: Secretly plan or try to achieve something; to allow something bad to happen.
Example: Some politicians connive at gambling.

Connotation
Meaning: The idea or feeling that a word evokes, beyond its literal meaning.
Example: For me, as a soldier, the word 'brotherhood' has a very positive connotation.

Construe
Meaning: To understand the meaning; make sense of.
Example: Different historians may construe the same historical event differently.

Contagious
Meaning: Spreads quickly; spread from one person to another.

Example: Fear is very contagious; this disease is highly contagious.

Contemplate
Meaning: Consider whether to do it or not.
Example: I'm contemplating going to France for a month.

Contravene
Meaning: Go against; to break the rule.
Example: His actions contravene the rules.

Conundrum
Meaning: Difficult problem or question.
Example: I have no answer to that conundrum.

Convergence
Meaning: When two separate elements join together or become similar.
Example: Converging roads; converging paths; converging opinions.

Convivial
Meaning: Pleasant; friendly; enjoyable.
Example: A convivial cocktail party.

Coruscant

Meaning: Sparkling; flashing; gleaming.

Example: Coruscant star; coruscant color.

Courteous

Meaning: Respectful; polite.

Example: Hotel staff must be courteous at all times.

Credulous

Meaning: Easily believe in something with little or no evidence.

Example: Credulous people always believe any TV advertisement.

Culpable

Meaning: Deserving blame; guilty; responsible for something bad.

Example: The judge found him culpable.

Curtail

Meaning: Reduce or limit something.

Example: You should try to curtail your expenses.

Debacle

Meaning: A powerful failure; fiasco.

Example: Her performance in the theater was a debacle.

Debase

Meaning: Reduce the value, status, or quality of something.

Example: Money has debased basketball.

Decimate

Meaning: To kill or destroy a large number of something.

Example: Decimate the population of exotic birds.

Deft

Meaning: Skillful; capable; clever; quick.

Example: The guitarist has deft fingers.

Delectable

Meaning: Delicious; attractive; tasteful.

Example: Delectable recipe; delectable meal; delectable lips.

Delineate

Meaning: Portray; accurately describe something; sketch out.

Example: Delineate the target; delineate characters; delineate the location.

Deluded

Meaning: To believe in something that is not real or true.

Example: We delude ourselves that we are in control.

Demure
Meaning: Shy; modest; bashful; quiet.
Example: He is always shy and demure with girls.

Denigrate
Meaning: To criticize someone hardly and unfairly; to spoil the reputation.
Example: Her terrible history denigrates her as a person.

Depute
Meaning: Transfer power to someone; allow someone to do something on your behalf.
Example: I have deputed my social media accounts to my manager.

Deride
Meaning: To criticize someone hardly, to laugh at someone.
Example: They deride her effort to get married as soon as possible.

Desecrate
Meaning: Deliberately damage something sacred, holy, or very much respected.
Example: The vandals desecrated the temple.

Deteriorate

Meaning: To become worse.

Example: Her health began to deteriorate.

Dexterous

Meaning: Very skillful and quick with their hands.

Example: Dexterous pianist; dexterous guitarist.

Digression

Meaning: Moving away from the main subject; turning aside.

Example: Digression from the main purpose of our meeting.

Discernment

Meaning: The ability to make good judgments.

Example: Anna shows good discernment in choosing friends.

Disclose

Meaning: To show what was hidden; to give out secret information to people.

Example: Disclose the details of a transaction; disclose your salary to colleagues.

Disconsolate

Meaning: Sad; unhappy; gloomy.

Example: Mary was disconsolate after her divorce.

Discrepancy

Meaning: The difference between two or more things that must be the same.

Example: A discrepancy between his public and private image.

Disdain

Meaning: Dislike someone or something; disrespect.

Example: Michael shows great disdain for the law.

Dislodge

Meaning: To remove something or someone from a position.

Example: Dislodge the rock; dislodge the Governor.

Disparage

Meaning: Express a negative opinion about someone or something.

Example: Don't disparage Mary's attempts to become a doctor.

Distraught

Meaning: Upset; sad; worried.

Example: My wife's death left me extremely distraught.

Docile

Meaning: Easily influenced or persuaded.

Example: Docile children; docile dogs.

Donnish
Meaning: Serious; smart; academic.
Example: He looks like a geek and donnish in manner.

Dour
Meaning: Antisocial; hard; unfriendly.
Example: He was a dour and gloomy man.

Dubious
Meaning: Not completely safe, true, or honest.
Example: Their claims were dubious and unproven.

Eagerly
Meaning: Enthusiastic about something; strong desire to have or do something.
Example: She's so eager to learn new language.

Ebullient
Meaning: Full of energy; positive.
Example: He was in ebullient mood.

Effete
Meaning: Weak; no longer capable; without power.
Example: Over the years, the king became effete.

Effrontery

Meaning: Bad behavior; extreme rudeness.

Example: He had the effrontery to ask for money after everything he had done to me.

Egalitarian

Meaning: Promotion of social equality and equal rights.

Example: Egalitarian society; this brand is not egalitarian.

Egregious

Meaning: Extremely bad.

Example: An egregious mistake; egregious behavior.

Eloquent

Meaning: Expressing what you mean using clear and efficient language.

Example: Eloquent speech; eloquent reminder.

Elucidate

Meaning: To clarify or explain something.

Example: Please elucidate this topic for me.

Embark

Meaning: To go onto a ship or to start doing something.

Example: He is about to embark on a lawyer career; embark on a boat trip.

Embellish
Meaning: To add details; to decorate.
Example: Please embellish your story with more details; I want to embellish my room with some flowers.

Embezzle
Meaning: To steal money.
Example: Anna was caught embezzling money from her parents.

Emboldened
Meaning: Give someone the courage to do something.
Example: I emboldened him to start a new business.

Empirical
Meaning: Based on observation or experience rather than theory.
Example: Empirical evidence; empirical studies; empirical analysis.

Enervating
Meaning: Tiring; exhausting.
Example: A hot climate enervates people.

Engulf

Meaning: To cover or surround something.

Example: The disease is threatening to engulf the entire country.

Enigma

Meaning: Mysterious or difficult to understand.

Example: She is an enigma to me.

Ennui

Meaning: Being tired or bored; having no interest in anything.

Example: I'm filled with sadness and ennui.

Ensue

Meaning: To happen after or as a result of something.

Example: A brief silence ensued.

Entreat

Meaning: To try hard to convince someone to do something.

Example: I entreat you to stop lying to me.

Entrenched

Meaning: Fixed; exist for a very long time.

Example: Greed is entrenched in our society.

Eradicate

Meaning: To destroy something completely.

Example: These diseases are very difficult to eradicate.

Erroneous

Meaning: Wrong; incorrect.

Example: Erroneous conclusions; erroneous assumptions; erroneous opinion.

Eschew

Meaning: Deliberately avoiding something.

Example: I want my son to eschew bad company.

Evasive

Meaning: To avoid telling the truth by not directly answering a question.

Example: He gave an evasive answer to my question.

Exacerbation

Meaning: Make something bad even worse.

Example: Exacerbation of the disease.

Exaggeration

Meaning: Presenting something in an excessive manner.

Example: She tends to exaggerate all her difficulties in life.

Excogitate

Meaning: To plan something; think out.

Example: To excogitate a method.

Exemplify

Meaning: Be a typical example of something.

Example: This painting perfectly exemplifies the Renaissance style.

Explicit

Meaning: Clear and detailed.

Example: I gave him explicit instructions on how to complete the project.

Expunge

Meaning: Remove completely.

Example: She want to expunge the incident from her memory.

Extemporize

Meaning: To improvise; perform or speak without any preparation.

Example: The lead actor forgot his lines and had to extemporize.

Facetious

Meaning: Trying to be funny and flippant in a serious situation.

Example: John was so facetious that he turned everything into a joke.

Fallacious
Meaning: Not correct; based on incorrect reasoning.
Example: Fallacious arguments; fallacious opinion.

Fastidious
Meaning: Very attentive to details.
Example: Jack was fastidious in his preparation for Barbara's birthday.

Fatuous
Meaning: Silly; stupid; pointless.
Example: This TV commercial is very fatuous.

Feasible
Meaning: Possible; able to be done.
Example: It's not feasible to complete your request.

Feral
Meaning: Wild; savage; existing in the wild.
Example: Feral animals.

Fervent
Meaning: Shows strong feelings about something.
Example: Fervent football supporter; fervent patriots.

Festive

Meaning: Having the spirit of a holiday or festival.

Example: Festive mood; festive holiday atmosphere.

Fiendish

Meaning: Cruel; unpleasant; evil; terribly complex.

Example: Fiendish crimes; fiendish language; fiendish task.

Flabbergasted

Meaning: Extremely surprised or shocked.

Example: My husband was flabbergasted when I announced my pregnancy.

Flagrant

Meaning: Shockingly obvious and bad.

Example: Flagrant violations; flagrant waste of money.

Flare up

Meaning: Sudden onset or increase, escalation.

Example: When he is afraid, his asthma always flares up.

Flinch

Meaning: Make a sudden movement as a reaction to pain or fear.

Example: She didn't even flinch when the nurse gave the injection.

Fluctuate

Meaning: To change frequently.

Example: Meat prices fluctuated.

Flummoxed

Meaning: Unable to understand; extremely confused.

Example: Dr. John was flummoxed by my symptoms.

Forbearance

Meaning: Self-control; patience.

Example: You must treat your little kid with forbearance.

Forthcoming

Meaning: About to happen.

Example: The forthcoming season.

Frenzy

Meaning: Uncontrolled and wild behavior; madness.

Example: In a frenzy of jealousy, she killed him.

Fret

Meaning: Constant worry or anxiety.

Example: John fretted about the rent.

Furtive

Meaning: Tries to avoid attention; secret; hidden.

Example: She furtively called her lover.

Galvanize

Meaning: To get someone to act by affecting or shocking them.

Example: To galvanize the students into studying hard.

Gloat

Meaning: Feel or express great pleasure due to one's own success or someone else's failure.

Example: Her enemies gloated over her failure.

Gobble

Meaning: To eat something hungrily or quickly; quickly use a large amount of something.

Example: John gobbled his dinner.

Grandiloquent

Meaning: A way of using language in a very sophisticated way to get attention and admiration.

Example: A grandiloquent speaker; grandiloquent language.

Gregarious

Meaning: Sociable; likes to be with other people.

Example: Our kids are highly gregarious.

Grieve
Meaning: Feeling of great sadness.
Example: I need time to grieve after my wife's death.

Groggy
Meaning: Feeling tired, weak, or confused.
Example: This sleeping pill made me feel very groggy.

Hackneyed
Meaning: Overused; lack of originality.
Example: Hackneyed phrase; hackneyed slogans.

Haughty
Meaning: Unfriendly; think you are better or smarter than others.
Example: She always speaks to me in a haughty tone.

Hectic
Meaning: Full of activity; very busy.
Example: Hectic day; hectic schedule.

Homage
Meaning: Deep respect for someone or something.
Example: To pay homage to veterans.

Hunt out

Meaning: Search until you find something.

Example: I hunted out my first book to show Jenna.

Ignominious

Meaning: Shameful; embarrassing.

Example: Ignominious failure; ignominious defeat.

Illicit

Meaning: Forbidden by law or rules.

Example: Illicit guns; illicit drugs.

Immense

Meaning: Extremely large or great.

Example: Immense pressure; immense power; immense amount.

Impeccable

Meaning: Perfect; of highest standards.

Example: She has impeccable taste in clothes.

Impecunious

Meaning: Poor; having little or no money.

Example: He is from impecunious family.

Impertinent

Meaning: Rude and disrespectful.

Example: Impertinent question; impertinent remark.

Impetuous

Meaning: Sudden; impulsive; rush.

Example: She may regret her impetuous decision.

Implore

Meaning: Beg someone to do something.

Example: I implore you not to leave me.

Inadvertent

Meaning: Accidental; not intentional; unwanted.

Example: Inadvertent misplacement; inadvertent error.

Incensed

Meaning: Very angry.

Example: She was incensed by the rising cost of education.

Incessant

Meaning: Continues without stopping.

Example: Incessant snowfall; incessant rain.

Inchoate

Meaning: Not yet properly developed; just started; partly formed.

Example: Inchoate plan; inchoate cancer.

Inconsequential

Meaning: Not important; trivial.

Example: Her work seems inconsequential.

Incumbent

Meaning: To have a certain official position.

Example: Incumbent President faces a tough fight for re-election next year.

Indelible

Meaning: Not able to be removed, forgotten, or erased.

Example: Indelible ink stain; indelible impression.

Indispensable

Meaning: Absolutely necessary.

Example: Smartphone is indispensable in modern life.

Indolent

Meaning: Lazy; wanting to avoid activity; slow; showing no interest.

Example: She is as indolent as her cat; indolent tumors; indolent reply.

Indubitable

Meaning: Something that can't be doubted; unquestionable.

Example: An indubitable truth; indubitable fact.

Inept
Meaning: Not skilled; not qualified; ineffective.
Example: He was an inept worker.

Inexorable
Meaning: Impossible to stop.
Example: Inexorable technological progress.

Inexplicable
Meaning: Impossible to explain.
Example: Her actions are completely inexplicable.

Inevitable
Meaning: Impossible to avoid or prevent.
Example: Their conflict was inevitable.

Infatuation
Meaning: A strong and short-living feeling of love.
Example: Her infatuation with him lasted one month.

Inimical
Meaning: Unfriendly; harmful; hostile; stop
something from progressing.
Example: Government actions are inimical to
economic growth.

Innate
Meaning: Something you were born with, natural.
Example: Innate sense of humor; innate talent.

Insatiable
Meaning: Impossible to satisfy.
Example: I have an insatiable lust for power.

Inscrutable
Meaning: Impossible to understand or interpret.
Example: An inscrutable face; inscrutable smile.

Insouciant
Meaning: Not worrying about possible problems; relaxed and happy; free from concern; carefree.
Example: He leads an insouciant life.

Interminable
Meaning: Seemingly endless.
Example: I'm tired of this interminable discussion; interminable stories of his baseball career.

Intransigent
Meaning: Refusal to compromise.
Example: Our company is intransigent and rejects all my ideas about innovation.

Intrepid

Meaning: Extremely brave; fearless.

Example: A squad of intrepid soldiers.

Intrinsic

Meaning: Essential; significant; extremely important.

Example: English language is an intrinsic part of the school curriculum.

Inveterate

Meaning: Habitual; one who does something extremely often.

Example: Inveterate gambler; inveterate smoker.

Invigorate

Meaning: To make someone feel fresh and full of energy.

Example: She was invigorated by the morning shower.

Irrevocable

Meaning: Impossible to change; final.

Example: Her decision is irrevocable.

Jaded

Meaning: Bored; tired; not happy.

Example: I felt extremely jaded after working all day.

Jarring
Meaning: Unexpected; unpleasant; shocking.
Example: Jarring sound; jarring note in her voice.

Jejune
Meaning: Very simple; dull; naive.
Example: Jejune behavior; jejune generalizations; jejune remark.

Jibe
Meaning: Rude and aggressive remark.
Example: He jibed constantly at the way she ran her company.

Jocular
Meaning: Humorous; playful.
Example: Jocular mood; jocular personality; jocular tone.

Jubilation
Meaning: A feeling of great happiness and triumph.
Example: The news about victory was greeted with jubilation.

Kitschy
Meaning: To be tasteless; ugly; without style.
Example: Kitschy culture; kitschy decorations.

Lash out

Meaning: Suddenly become aggressive or attack someone.

Example: He lashed out and knocked out my teeth.

Laudable

Meaning: Deserves praise or admiration.

Example: A laudable performance; laudable effort.

Lingers

Meaning: Takes a long time to disappear or die; gradually disappearing or dying.

Example: The smell of your perfume always lingers on my shirt.

Loquacious

Meaning: The one who talks a lot.

Example: Loquacious comedian.

Lousy

Meaning: Poor; of a very bad quality; disgusting.

Example: I'm lousy at baseball; the food was lousy.

Lucrative

Meaning: Profitable; making a lot of money.

Example: My business is very lucrative.

Ludicrous
Meaning: Stupid; foolish; unreasonable.
Example: Ludicrous idea; ludicrous joke.

Lushy (Slang word in American English)
Meaning: Drunk; beery; alcoholic.

Maddening
Meaning: Makes you feel angry; extremely annoying.
Example: Maddening habit; maddeningly slow.

Magic away
Meaning: Make something disappear.
Example: I wish I could magic us away from this boring lesson.

Mediocre
Meaning: Of average quality.
Example: Her new book was pretty mediocre.

Mendacious
Meaning: Lying; not telling the truth.
Example: These statements are mendacious; her arguments are mendacious.

Mercurial
Meaning: Changes suddenly or unpredictably.
Example: A mercurial temperament.

Misdemeanor

Meaning: Not so serious crime; a minor wrongdoing.

Example: The player was disqualified for a drug misdemeanor.

Modicum

Meaning: A small amount of something.

Example: He is a bad doctor without a modicum of medical knowledge.

Morbid

Meaning: Unhealthy interest in unpleasant topics, such as death or illness.

Example: Dan has a morbid fascination with blood.

Mundane

Meaning: Ordinary; commonplace; not interesting.

Example: Her job is very mundane.

Munificent

Meaning: Very generous.

Example: He donated a munificent amount of money to charity.

Myriad

Meaning: Extremely great amount of something.

Example: Myriad of problems; myriad of options.

Negligent

Meaning: Unable to properly take care of anything; careless.

Example: Dr. Bob was negligent in her duties.

Nibble

Meaning: Take small bites out.

Example: She nibbled a croissant.

Nimble

Meaning: Fast and light in motion.

Example: Nimble fingers; nimble tongue.

Nonchalant

Meaning: Calm and relaxed.

Example: John is completely nonchalant about his future.

Obliterate

Meaning: Completely destroy something.

Example: Dan tried to obliterate the memory of the accident.

Obloquy

Meaning: Strong public criticism.

Example: The president's admission of adultery caused an obloquy among voters.

Obsequious

Meaning: Too eager to help or agree with someone.

Example: Mike is obsequious to all those in power.

Obsolete

Meaning: Outdated; no longer used.

Example: His work is now obsolete because of the machines.

Obstreperous

Meaning: Noisy; aggressive; difficult to control.

Example: An obstreperous child.

Ominous

Meaning: To assume that something bad might happen.

Example: Ominous dark clouds; ominous silence.

Opulent

Meaning: Wealthy; rich; luxurious.

Example: Opulent lifestyle; opulent house.

Ostensible

Meaning: Seems true, but not necessarily.

Example: Ostensible reason; ostensible ownership; ostensible purpose.

Outrageous
Meaning: Extremely bad; morally unacceptable.
Example: I must apologize for my outrageous behavior.

Overt
Meaning: Open; not hidden.
Example: An overt act of aggression; overt criticism.

Pal around
Meaning: Spend time with someone as a friend.
Example: I used to pal around with her in college.

Parsimonious
Meaning: Not willing to spend money.
Example: He is too parsimonious to buy a second laptop for work.

Paucity
Meaning: Small amount; not enough of something.
Example: There's a paucity of skilled workers.

Penitent
Meaning: Show that you are sorry for something bad that you did.
Example: He is deeply penitent.

Peremptory

Meaning: Expect other people to accept something immediately and without question; not open to appeal.

Example: Peremptory instructions; peremptory in tone; peremptory commands.

Perfidious

Meaning: Unfaithful; unable to be trusted.

Example: Our company was betrayed by perfidious employees.

Perfunctory

Meaning: Done without much care, attention, or interest.

Example: The police made a perfunctory search of the house.

Perky

Meaning: Happy and cheerful.

Example: Their child is so perky.

Pernicious

Meaning: Dangerous; harmful.

Example: Cigarettes are pernicious to the health.

Perpetual

Meaning: Lasts forever; never ending.

Example: Perpetual constitution; perpetual license.

Pertain to
Meaning: Connected with; related to; refer to.
Example: Her remark did not pertain to the topic.

Pompous
Meaning: Someone who thinks he is too important or serious.
Example: Pompous rhetoric; pompous politician.

Precise
Meaning: Exact; accurate.
Example: Precise date; precise information.

Promulgate
Meaning: To spread; make something widely known.
Example: Promulgate the belief; promulgate information.

Propitious
Meaning: Shows a good chance of success.
Example: It was a propitious time to launch their new game.

Protracted
Meaning: Lasting for a long time.

Example: Protracted dispute; protracted negotiations.

Puerile
Meaning: Childish; silly.
Example: She has a puerile sense of humor.

Pugnacious
Meaning: Ready to argue or fight; aggressive.
Example: Mike gets very pugnacious when he drinks.

Querulous
Meaning: Annoying; often complaining.
Example: He complained in a querulous voice; querulous old man.

Quirky
Meaning: Unique in an interesting way.
Example: His sense of humor was quite quirky.

Quixotic
Meaning: Super-idealistic and unrealistic.
Example: His plan to become the richest man on the planet was quixotic.

Rancorous
Meaning: Hateful; angry.
Example: Rancorous dispute; rancorous attack.

Ravage
Meaning: To damage or ruin something.
Example: Our house was ravaged by the flood.

Ravishing
Meaning: Extremely beautiful and attractive.
Example: She looked so ravishing in that dress.

Recalcitrant
Meaning: Unwilling to obey orders.
Example: Recalcitrant children; recalcitrant workers.

Recluse
Meaning: Living alone; avoiding the company of other people.
Example: Many creative people are recluses.

Recondite
Meaning: Difficult or impossible to understand.
Example: This article is full of recondite information.

Reluctant
Meaning: Unwilling to do something.
Example: He was reluctant to work.

Replete
Meaning: Extremely full.
Example: She was replete with food.

Repudiate

Meaning: Claim that something is not true; refuse to accept.

Example: Repudiate evidence; repudiate a contract.

Resplendent

Meaning: Bright; attractive; impressive.

Example: She was resplendent in that skirt.

Reticent

Meaning: Someone who doesn't want to talk about their feelings.

Example: She is very reticent about her past.

Revitalize

Meaning: To give something new life.

Example: Revitalize our society; revitalize your energy.

Rubicon

Meaning: Point of no return.

Example: Today I crossed the Rubicon and now there is no going back.

Sagacious

Meaning: Smart and able to make the right decisions.

Example: Sagacious businessman; sagacious old man.

Sanguine

Meaning: Cheerful; optimistic; confident.

Example: He is sanguine about his future.

Scintillating

Meaning: Brilliantly clever; shining; skillful.

Example: Scintillating mind; scintillating jewelers.

Scruffy

Meaning: Messy; dirty.

Example: Scruffy T-shirt.

Searing

Meaning: Very hot or intense.

Example: Searing heat; searing pain.

Shenanigans

Meaning: Secret or dishonest activities.

Example: Business shenanigans.

Shrewd

Meaning: Able to judge people and situations clearly.

Example: John is a shrewd businessman.

Simmer down

Meaning: Become peaceful or less angry.

Example: Simmer down and stop hitting him!

Sluggish

Meaning: Slow-moving; not energetic; inactive.

Example: Heavy breakfast makes me sluggish.

Soothing

Meaning: Making you feel calm and relaxed.

Example: Soothing voice; soothing music.

Sordid

Meaning: Dirty; dishonest; nasty.

Example: Sordid business; sordid affairs.

Squeamish

Meaning: Easily made to feel sick or disgusted.

Example: I'm terribly squeamish about blood.

Squander

Meaning: To waste money in a foolish manner.

Example: Don't squander your money on an unnecessary fifth car.

Surreptitiously

Meaning: Done secretly; by stealth.

Example: Mike surreptitiously passed him exam answers.

Tatty

Meaning: In a bad condition; old.

Example: Tatty old jacket.

Tentative
Meaning: Not certain; not fixed.
Example: Tentative conclusions; tentative report.

Tenuous
Meaning: Very weak; unsure.
Example: Tenuous connection; tenuous evidence.

Timid
Meaning: Shy; without much confidence.
Example: Every time John sees Mary, he acts like a timid child.

Titivate
Meaning: To make more attractive.
Example: Titivate her costume with some accessories.

Treacherous
Meaning: Most likely to betray; very dangerous; difficult to deal with.
Example: Your ex best friend's treacherous intentions to reveal all your secrets; treacherous weather; treacherous road; treacherous path; treacherous hike.

Trespass

Meaning: Break into someone's property without permission.

Example: He was trespassing on private property.

Turmoil

Meaning: A state of intense anxiety, confusion, or uncertainty.

Example: After the crisis, the country was in turmoil.

Turpitude

Meaning: Wickedness; amoral behavior.

Example: Moral turpitude.

Ubiquitous

Meaning: Seems to be everywhere.

Example: A ubiquitous fashion.

Ulterior

Meaning: Intentionally hidden; secret.

Example: Ulterior purpose; ulterior motives.

Unparagoned

Meaning: Having no analogues; incomparable.

Example: Unparagoned recipe; unparagoned sense of style.

Unhinge

Meaning: To make someone mentally unstable.

Example: The stress completely unhinged her.

Vacillate

Meaning: To waver between two options or opinions.

Example: This time, she did not vacillate and accepted the offer.

Valiant

Meaning: Showing courage or determination.

Example: Valiant knight; valiant effort.

Venal

Meaning: Corrupt; prone to bribery.

Example: Venal policeman; venal judge.

Verbose

Meaning: Containing more words than necessary.

Example: Verbose explanation; verbose report.

Vigilant

Meaning: Careful and watchful, especially to avoid danger.

Example: He tried to be vigilant and report anything suspicious.

Virulent

Meaning: Dangerous; harmful in its effects.

Example: Virulent infection; virulent disease; virulent media campaign against him.

Vociferous

Meaning: Speaks loudly and with great energy.

Example: He was a vociferous speaker.

Voracious

Meaning: Want a lot of something.

Example: He was a voracious stamp-collector.

Wreathe

Meaning: To cover, encircle, or surround something.

Example: The clouds wreathed the hills; she was wreathed in smoke.

Printed in Great Britain
by Amazon

85538286R00037